D0690532

Do not let anyone rob you of your shine.

OTHER BOOKS BY ROBERT M. DRAKE

Spaceship (2012)

The Great Artist (2012)

Science (2013)

Beautiful Chaos (2014)

Beautiful Chaos 2 (2014)

Black Butterfly (2015)

A Brilliant Madness (2015)

Beautiful and Damned (2016)

Broken Flowers (2016)

Gravity: A Novel (2017)

Star Theory (2017)

Chaos Theory (2017)

Light Theory (2017)

Moon Theory (2017)

Dead Pop Art (2017)

Chasing The Gloom: A Novel (2017)

Moon Matrix (2018)

Seeds of Wrath (2018)

Dawn of Mayhem (2018)

The King is Dead (2018)

For Excerpts and Updates please follow:

Instagram.com/rmdrk
Facebook.com/rmdrk
Twitter.com/rmdrk

THE KING IS DEAD *copyright* © 2018 by
Robert M. Drake. All rights reserved.

Printed in U.S.A. No part of this book may
be used or reproduced in any manner
whatsoever without written permission
except in the case of reprints in the context
of reviews.

ISBN: 978-1-7326900-3-5

Book Cover: Robert M. Drake
Cover Image licensed by Shutter Stock Inc.

For The Unhappy.

CONTENTS

THE KING IS DEAD

ROBERT M. DRAKE

THE WORST PART

The worst part is,
they won't appreciate your worth

until you're gone
and sadly,

they'll realize this
when it's too late

and when you've already
moved on.

When you've already
found someone

you deserve.

DROWNING

If they love you
they won't give up

on you.

Period.

They'll try to save you...

even if they end up
drowning themselves.

SO HARSH

I'm sorry to be
so harsh

but you only live once
and your time

shouldn't be spent
on anyone

who doesn't love themselves.

So take this as a sign,
it's time to move on...

and don't try
to convince yourself
to stay.

Because you don't deserve it,
no one does.

So set them free,
trust the process...

letting go
can be a beautiful thing—
a refreshing thing.

Just before you go,
hope the best for them

and pray God grants them
the peace

they deserve.

HONESTY

Honesty is rare.

When you find it
cherish it.

Hold it with tender hands
and don't take it

for granted
especially for something

you know won't last.

ART & ARTIST

I make art.

I make sacrifices.

And I love
with the purest intention.

I don't want to hurt
another human being.

I don't want to cause them
any pain. I refuse to.

What I hope for is simple:

Peace and clarity.
Focus and hustle.

I work hard.

I don't let my feelings
stop me.

I do what I do
because I must.

So sound the alarm.
Alert the country.

Alert the broken
and the ones who break
the laws.

The rebels
and the game changers.

This is my art.
This is my story.

And this is my pain.

I want to love you
but I cannot...

instead I'll love you
where it hurts

the most.

THE FACTS

Sometimes
you have to accept the fact

that they didn't love you...

and move on.

Sometimes
you just realize
when it's time to let go

and pick yourself back up—
to piece everything

they broken
back together again.

STRONG WILLED

We don't have to
let each other go

because we don't agree
on some things.

We don't have to
argue or not speak

to each other
for a few days.

I have my beliefs
and you have yours.

We can take a moment
of silence to gather

our thoughts
and settle our emotions

but we don't have to
break up over a disagreement.

Let's work on it, baby.

Let's make the best
of it and move on.

We're both strong willed people
and we're both stubborn

at times

but we have big hearts to give.

And I want you
and I know you want me.

We just have to look past
what hurts

and build
on what we know

we already have.

SELF-HEALING

I'm still trying to move on
from the things

I don't like to talk about.

I'm still trying
to live—knowing

I wasn't as important
to you

as I once thought
I was.

HOLD ME

You hold me
because sometimes

I feel like falling apart

and I hold you
because sometimes

it makes me feel
like I'm in the safest place

in the world.

NOTHING WRONG

There's nothing wrong
with taking things slow—

with trying to get to know you
and be your friend.

We don't have to go through
the process so fast.

I want to be your friend
before I become your lover.

I want to know you,
so I can be real with you.

So I could give you
the kind of love

I know
you deserve.

DIFFERENCES

We don't heal
the same way

therefore

we must always remember
to be kind.

Everyone is hurting
and everyone is healing

the best way
they know how.

DOUBLE LOOK

I can't find it in my heart
to do you wrong.

There's no revenge
in me.

You broke me
and I learned from it.

I moved on
and I never looked back

twice.

IT IS HARD NOT TO CARE

When you really care for them
and have a connection

with them

it's really hard
to move on.

It's really hard
to see past what you've built.

But some bridges
are meant to be broken down

and some pathways
are forever...

and if it's meant to be,
they'll always find their way back home.

Just remember
to follow your heart,

trust where it leads you
and if they really belong to you,

then

they will return to you.

So be patient,
let the past go

and be ready
when they arrive.

PROTECT YOUR...

Protect your energy
because
there are so many things

that could break you.

So don't let
what brings you

inner peace
be one of them.

COULD BECOME

Maybe I'm too nice
or maybe I'm just a sucker...

but I have this bad habit
of trusting people.

Of giving them my all.

Maybe I'm blinded

by love
and affection

or maybe I want to see
the good in them

no matter what.

I let people in
too quickly

and I have this curse
of seeing pass who they are—
what they've done

and believing
in who they could *become*.

MIND GAMES

I don't have time to play
these mind games.

I've got a caring heart.

I've been through hell
and I'm ready to love.

Take it or leave it.

Don't waste my time
or yours.

We're too grown
to fuck either up.

Let's give it a try
or none at all.

The choice is yours.

I WONDER

I sometimes wonder
what I mean to you.

What you feel
when I'm holding you

and what goes through
your mind

when I'm gone.

IT IS A COLD WORLD

We live in a cold world.

We shouldn't have to
convince people
to be kind.

We shouldn't have to
remind them to love.

We are surrounded
by humans with no humanity.

By lovers
who don't know how to love.

By leaders
who cannot lead

and by preachers
who hold no gospel to preach.

By artists
who do not understand their art.

And by brothers
and sisters

who neglect their families.

This is how it burns.
This is how it ends.

This is how we evolve
out of touch.

Out of soul.

Our brains are wired
and our hearts are slowly eaten away.

The world is cold
and we are getting colder...

and the wars are spreading faster
and the injustice is becoming

more of the norm.

The killings
and the murders.

And the fighters
and the lovers.

We stay.
We stay.
We stay.

And all of us remain
and all of us are still,

and all of us search
for the truth of light…

of the *dying light,*
of the *dying word.*

We live in a cold world,
there's no doubt about it

but we shouldn't have to convince
each other

that we are worthy
of love.

Of holding it.
Of finding it.

And sharing it,
with one another

at all cost.

NO TIME

I don't have time
to cry over you.

I'm sorry, baby
I just don't.

Right now
it's all about me...

but nonetheless,
I'll pray for you.

And I hope
God grants you peace,

spiritual growth and answers...

for all the questions
you've been asking

yourself lately.

NOT ALL

Not all love
is good love

and not all energy
is good energy.

And just because
they love you,

doesn't give them the right
to disrespect you...

doesn't give them the right
to belittle you.

No one is doing you any favors
and you definitely don't

owe anyone anything.

So if it doesn't feel like home
then you have the right to leave.

You don't have to stay
if you don't want to

and you don't have to pretend
you're on good terms

just to show face.

People separate all the time.

They break-up over anything—
over nothing

but let it be known,
you don't have to take the verbal abuse.

You don't have to put up with it...
and you shouldn't worry about

the consequences.

I'd be more concerned
if you stayed,

if you didn't have the courage
to do anything about it.

So take this with you...

take this as a sign
and as a lesson.

Those who don't respect you
will never respect you.

No matter how much time
you give them.

No matter how many nights you pray
for them to change.

Like I said,

not all love
is good love

and not all energy
is good energy

but you should know the difference
between who deserves your loyalty

and who doesn't.

Between who deserves your time
and who doesn't

and know how to respond
to it as well.

Only you know what type of love

you deserve.

Only you.

Remember that.

NEVER ASK FOR MUCH

You don't ask for much
but you deserve a lot.

The same way
you underestimate your value

and deal with all the bullshit
some people bring.

INSIDE OF YOU

Whatever you believe in...

know

that God will always
have your back

even if you don't
have his.

Know

that God believes in you
and what's in your heart,

even if you don't
believe in him.

Know

that when you want revenge,
God will give you peace.

Know

that whenever it hurts,
God will give you growth
and time.

Know

that whenever you fail,
God will give you experience.

Know

that whenever you feel
like ending it all,

God will give you
the strength you need

to carry on.

God got you.

Let the rest pan out
on its own.

There comes a time
in our lives

when we must let go
and let in.

Let go and let God.

LITTLE THINGS

It is the little things
 you take with you

when they're gone—
the details you never seemed

to notice.

Like the first time you kissed
and the last time

you looked
into their eyes.

DO NOT FORCE IT

Don't force love to happen...

let it happen.

Not everyone
will have the same

intensity as you.

You can't grow a garden
without sunlight

and you can't keep them alive
without pouring

the right amount of water.

Don't rush it,
let it be.

It is a privilege
to love

and be loved.

So please,
don't turn it into a job.

Let it happen,
and if it is meant to be

then it shall
and if not,

then let it go.

It's simple.
That's all.

LOVE HER

You want to love her
but you're too

into your friends

and you're too
into giving your attention

to other women.

You tell her you care
but you're barely around

to spend time with her.

You tell her you're busy,
that you'll make it up to her

but you never get around in doing so.

And then you tell her
you're loyal.

That she's the *only one*
in your life.

Then you tell her
you want her,

that she's all you need
but you don't put the effort in.

This you must learn

and *you will*
when she is gone.

You're not a lover, my sweet friend.

You're a liar.

So please don't confuse the two.

And please
stop telling her

who you want her
to think you are.

You're not ready.
Do not waste her time.

Now carry on.

WATERING YOURSELF

Don't water yourself down
because someone doesn't

have the time
to understand you.

If someone wants
to be there for you,

then they'll make the effort
to break you down.

It's one of those things
you know

and not
one of those things
you'll question

down the road.

APOLOGY

You have my apology
but you don't have my trust.

You might have
fooled me once

but you will *never*
fool me twice.

I won't let you drown
but I will leave you

stranded

in the ocean forever.

LETTING GO

Stop holding on to people
who don't care about you.

It's hard to move forward
with a *fucking* mountain

weighing on your shoulder.

THE LAWS

What comes around
goes around.

You reap
what you sow.

You can't expect to spread lies
and be surrounded by loyalty.

You can't treat people wrong
and expect others

to do you right.

You get
what you put out.

You can't cause chaos
and expect to be surrounded

by peace and love.

THE KING IS DEAD

Stop going back to them.

Stop believing in the excuses.

In the promises.
In the lies.

People don't change
overnight.

They don't change
over an argument,

over an apology.

People *don't change* like that.

They don't learn
to appreciate you like that.

That is,
if you keep taking them back

and keep making it easy
for them to return—easy

for them not to change
or grow

or understand
what it is they've done.

I've said this before,
some people are good with words.

Some people will make you believe
in what they're saying

and not in
what they're doing.

Don't take this lightly,

but the realist thing anyone can do
is keep their word—

back up their apologies
with actions

and hold up to their promises
with effort.

Anything else
should be taken with a grain of salt.

Anything else
isn't worth your time.

You deserve someone
who isn't going to bullshit you.

Someone

who stays true
to their word.

And someone

who's willing to rebuild with you...

without letting
your kingdom fall.

GIVE ME PEACE (ONLY)

You deserve peace
but all you get is chaos.

The same way

you deserve love
but you always seem

to find yourself

hurting
a little more.

FOR EVERYTHING

Don't ever think

the tears
and the sleepless nights

are for nothing.

Sometimes
you have to cry
and go through hell

to move on.

SENSITIVE

I'm a sensitive, guy
what could I say.

I want to see people
for who they can become

rather than
who they are.

So whether you love me
or hate me.

I want to believe
in the greater good

because

I know at some point
you had a good heart.

I know at some point
someone did you wrong.

Someone *really*
fucked you over.

Someone *really*
turned your heart

into stone.

So I want people
to believe in you.

I want to look past
what you've done

and give you another chance.

Give you another shot
at love.

Because you deserve someone
who can bring out

the soft side in you.

You deserve someone
who could make you laugh,

someone

who could make you sit back
and wonder.

Someone
who's capable of filling the emptiness

in your soul.
The rough parts

in your heart.

Because you've been through enough.

Isn't it time for
you to surrender to someone

who wants to be there
for you.

Someone,
you can be yourself with.

I know it's hard to believe in people
and in their words

but at least
let me prove it to you.

Let me remind you
of who you once were.

Let's make it happen
because we have everything to gain

and nothing to lose.

Let's do this.

Take my hand,
let me show you the world

how you've never seen it before.

Let me reset your eyes
and set your soul on fire.

Let me love you
and let's become

all the things
we never received.

SOME PEOPLE

Some people
are just too hard

to deal with.

No matter how real
you are with them.

Some people
will take their insecurities

and throw it back at you.

They'll make you look crazy
no matter how hard

you're trying
to help.

LOST WORDS

It's sad to say
but sometimes

you have to purposely
ignore them.

You have to forward
their calls,

avoid the places they go to
and block out

their friends completely.

Sometimes
you have to be cold

to move on.

You have to treat them
how they treated you

and that's what hurts
the most.

EXPECTATIONS ON RISE

Don't expect anyone
to save you.

Don't expect anyone
to have all the answers

to your questions.

If there is something
I can write

or say to save a life
then it is this:

No one can save you
but yourself.

All you have to do
is put the work in.

Anything and everything

can be accomplished
with a little dedication

and love.

BROKEN HEART STRINGS

You play with everyones heart
but here's one thing

you won't see coming.

One day

you will find yourself in pieces.

You will find yourself
laying in the darkness.

You will find yourself
regretting all the damage you've caused,

especially
to those who love you.

And when that day comes
you won't be playing anyone

but yourself.

You won't be playing games anymore
and what is sad is,

how no one will take you seriously.
No one will be by your side.

It's harsh to say,
and I don't want to be

the bad guy to say this
or to even think it.

But one day,

you will give your heart to someone
and you will finally understand

what it's like
to have it returned back to you

split in two.

You will finally understand
what it's like to bleed

and to bleed
without any clotting.

And you might weep.

You might be still.
And you might die

but if you don't change you attitude
toward people,

then no one will be there

to help you.

No one will be there
to comfort you

as your heart breaks
and slowly

slips away.

I'm sorry,
that's just the way it is.

NOT WEAK

Being sensitive
doesn't make you weak.

Some of the strongest people
I've met

have the softest hearts.

They feel the deepest
and feel connected

to it all.

ONE FACT

Here is one fact
I've learned about people.

Most demand the truth
but when the truth comes out

not many are prepared
to deal with it.

So please
don't sugarcoat it for me.

I want the truth
in all rawness

about how you feel.

About what you want
and don't want.

And don't be sensitive about it.

Spew it out
like a hot cannon.

Let it go.

I only want facts, baby

and I want them
even if it hurts.

AMEN.

THE OTHER SIDE OF YOU

People bring out
different sides of you,

therefore,

you should always
keep the ones

who bring out
the light.

ABOUT THE WOMEN

These men say
they're all about their women

until it's time to step up

for their women.

Until it's time
to heal their women,

empower their women.

Keep your head up, sis.

Don't be fooled by a man
who doesn't know your worth.

Just keep your emotions
to yourself for now.

Get your heart and mind right

and *stay elevated.*

Everything soon will fall
into place.

I promise.

MOVING ON

They tell you to move on
but something's are easier said

than done
and to be honest

some people are just
too damn unforgettable.

Some people touch your soul
in ways

you could never imagine.

And sadly,
some people awaken

a love so deep within you
that no amount of time

can ever
ease your soul..

THE LIGHT

The truth will always
come out.

So if they lie to you
and deny it,

give it time
and be patient

and wait

till it all unfolds.

ATTENTION IS A KILLER

Don't let it get to your head.

Attention is not love.

Controlling someone
is not love.

Making people do
what you want

is not love.

Don't let it confuse your heart.

When it's love
you'll feel it, know it

and you won't
have to question

a damn thing.

TELL ME, TELL YOU

And they will tell you
how much they love you.

They will tell you
how beautiful you are

to them
and how special

you make them feel.

And they will flood your heart
with these ideas

and feelings.

And you will believe them,
not because you are naive

but because
you want to believe in love.

Because you want to believe
in their words—

in their fallacies.

And believe,

that they will be pretty.

They will be sweet
and they will lift you onto the air

but will not be strong enough
to keep you there.

Because after awhile
words have no weight

without action.

After awhile
words become dull

and dim
without effort.

The struggle is real

and finding someone
who'll be true to their word

is rare.

So if they show you how they feel
without contradiction,

then keep them.
Love them.

Protect them
and continue to do so.

You must.

Actions are much more beautiful
than words.

So look for them.

Pay attention to them
and hold on to them.

Whoever shows you this,
please don't be afraid

to love them most.

Don't be afraid

to love them hard.

They are of your same tribe
and you must always find those

who make you feel
at home.

TO YOURSELF

You have to
prove it to yourself.

No one is going to save you
from the fire.

No one is going to walk you
through the darkness.

No one is going to help you
from drowning.

Everyone is going through
their own struggle—

through their own personal hell.

Everyone is too busy
trying to fix themselves.

You have to
hold your own hand

sometimes

and not count on anyone
but yourself...

and not let anyone

rob you
of your shine.

THE PAST STILL HURTS

And I'm still
getting over my past...

but I will tell you this,

your friendship has made it
a lot easier for me

to move on
and I'm grateful

for what we have.

So thank you for everything.

Thank you for all
the long talks—

for listening to me

when I was breaking down.

And thank you
for bringing the sun with you—

during the times
I was drowning in the rain.

A LOT LEFT

Yeah,

I still have
a lot of growing up

to do
but that doesn't mean

I don't know about love.

That doesn't mean
I don't hurt just as bad

as you do
or cry
or feel.

Age makes no difference
and sometimes

you live through something
so devastating—you have *no choice*

but to grow up.

GRATEFUL

We're not going to agree
with everything

that's happened

but it made us
who we are today

and for that
I'm grateful.

Thank you.

THAT PLACE

Find that place
that sets your soul on fire.

Breathe there.
Grow there.
Love there.

It doesn't have to be
an actual place.

It does not have to be
another person.

Find that place
that sets your soul on fire.

It can be a memory.
It can be a song.

It can be your solitude.

It can be the sound
of your breathing

or the sound
of the wind.

Find that place

that sets your soul on fire.

Find it
and get lost there.

Find it
and live there

and show others
how to get there.

Find that place
that sets your soul on fire.

Risk everything
for this place.

Protect this place.
Die for this place.

Find yourself
and what you love

in this place.

It dwells in you.

This place.
This fire.

The stars are burning

in the middle of the night

and

so are you…

NEVER DO

Don't apologize
for being who you are.

It takes years
to be comfortable

with yourself
and years

to realize
that the opinions of others
do not matter.

Don't apologize, never do.

Keep shining.

FEEL THE SAME

You will know
who is important to you

from the moment
they leave,

because

when they do,
nothing ever seems

to feel the same.

UNDERSTAND THIS

Is it hard to understand
that I don't want a lover.

I'm not looking for one.

Why can't I be vulnerable
with someone, gentle with someone,

without making them believe
I want more.

I want a friend.

Someone I can be myself with.
Someone I could vent to.

Someone I can depend on—
lean on, when I need it most.

Someone who isn't afraid
to hurt my feelings

or tell me when I'm wrong.

Is it that hard to find?

As if finding a lover
isn't already hard enough,

so why is finding someone
I could open up to

even harder.

Everyone is so goddamn sensitive
and almost everyone

I've met
can't invest their time

into someone
without expecting some kind

of relationship
on their terms, too.

I'm not looking for a lover—
for a romantic relationship.

I don't need one,
at least not right now.

I just want a friend goddamnit!

Someone I can trust.

Someone I can feel free with
and not have to worry

about hurting their feelings.

I just want someone
to be there for me

and show me what
true friendship

is all about

when I feel
like I'm breaking apart.

That's all.

BEEN THROUGH

After everything we've been through.

All the good times.
All the memories.

All the beautiful moments
we created.

We should not
let it end like this.

We should not
let our egos

and pride
get in the way.

What's done
is done

and we shouldn't
make things harder

than they
already are.

I still want you
and I still have so many feelings

for you.

So let's not make this something
we'll regret.

Let's not throw it away
over nothing, baby.

I don't have anything else to say.

I'm not ready to move on
or let go.

I love you,
I really fucking love you

and I'm willing to go to the moon
and back

to make things work.

Let's hold on
for a little while longer

until we make sense
of everything

that hurts.

GROWN APART

We've grown apart
and it is sad to say

that the person I once loved
is someone

I no longer relate to.

Someone
I don't know anymore.

I hope you find
what you're looking for

and I hope you find
and chase

all the things
that make you feel free.

NEVER APART

I admit

I was wrong
and I pray to God

I never lose you

because

I just want to love you
like we've never

been hurt
at all.

IT IS IMPORTANT

Your mental health is important.

Therefore,
you should be with someone

who knows how to deal with you
when you're feeling sad

or blue.

Someone who knows
how to ease the pain—

how to bring you back
when you've drifted, too far.

Through good
or bad times,

find someone who adds
to your peace

and not to the chaos
in your mind
and heart.

After all,
your mental health

is important

and you need someone
who brings light

and not someone
who'll bury you deeper

in the darkness
of your heart.

I CANNOT SAY NO

I wasn't done with you

but I still held the door
as you walked away.

So I'm speaking this
into existence.

I want you
and I don't care

about the past anymore.

I don't care
about the way we hurt
each other.

Let bygones be bygones.

And let
the universe of us

grow

like it's something
we can't replace.

TOO MUCH OF NOTHING

I feel too much.

I stress too much.
I overthink too much.

I know it's not the way
I should be living my life

but there are some things
I can't control.

I feel too much.
I hurt too much.

I love too much.

And sometimes
there's no need to.

I can't help it,
this is who I am.

Bones.
Skin.

Soul.
Heart and all.

And how you treat me
is how you feel about me

and you either understand me
for who I am

or you don't
at all.

NO BEGGARS HERE

Never beg anyone to stay.

You're better than that, baby.

Just make sure
to open the door

for them
when they leave

and shut it
once they're gone.

There's nothing wrong
with knowing your worth

and nothing wrong
with moving on.

STAY REAL

Stay real, baby.

You don't have to be
perfect for someone.

You don't have to be
enough either.

And you definitely don't
have to pretend

to be someone else
for them.

Just be yourself.

Accept your flaws—
work in them.

And remember,

not to waste your time
on anyone

who doesn't appreciate you.

How they treat you
is how they feel about you

and you should never
fuck with anyone

who has never had
their heart broken,

for they have so much
to learn about people

and also,
themselves.

LOVE YOU

Allow the people
who love you

to love you.

There's nothing
more beautiful

than knowing
how someone feels

and letting them show you

how much
they care.

THE BREAKS

Some heartbreaks
can save you.

They can really
turn your life around

and *change* it
for the best.

SOMETHING NEW IS OLD

You should never
hold on to anyone

who doesn't want
to be held

or anyone
who doesn't want to stay.

Pay attention.

You'll know
by their actions

and you'll know
when it's time to let go.

Even if it hurts
your life will correct itself

when it has to.

It will always
cut off the loose ends

to make room
for something new.

MATTER'S MOST

Maybe it was your fault
or maybe it wasn't

but it's not like it matters.

What matters is
taking the time you need

on yourself
now that you're alone.

Giving yourself
what you need to heal.

To move on.
To grow from the experience.

So maybe it was
your fault

or maybe it wasn't.

Take advantage of this moment
because it's *your* moment

and right now
everything looks

a hell of a lot brighter
than before.

Never look back,

the world can still be yours
as long as you believe

in what matters most.

GIVE ME THE SEA

You cannot love me
to then get rid of me.

That's not the way it works.

You cannot give me
a drop of water

and expect me to survive
after you've given me

the sea.

FLAWS OF MINE

You can't use
my flaws against me.

I know I'm broken.

I know sometimes
I go through depression

and I know
my stress is real

but that won't stop me.

You won't stop me
because I believe in myself

and not in your words.

I believe in what I can do
and not in what you think

I can't do.

I'm better now.

I'm stronger now
and there isn't a say

that could tell me otherwise.

It's too late to convince me
that I'm no good.

I'm no stranger to my heart.

I know who I am
and I know what I'm capable of.

Amen.

WRONG PERSON

One day
it will all make sense.

One day
you will realize

how your love was enough
and you were just spending it

on the wrong person.

That's all.

PREACH WHAT YOU LOVE

They preach love.

They preach peace.
They preach togetherness.

Nowadays
everyone seems
to want to heal someone.

Everyone seems
to want to help.

And some do help.

Some really pour their hearts
into other people.

Really save them, too.

But then
there are some who preach
the same things.

Who teach
and want to understand

the world for what it is.

Then,
they will throw shade
to someone they don't know

the moment they feel
a threat.

I don't understand these people.

They preach love
to only express hate

when someone doesn't
agree with them.

They preach peace
but only display war

when someone
isn't on their side.

They preach togetherness
to only separate themselves

when someone isn't a part
of their tribe.

These people.
These sides.
These divisions.

Some people don't know
what to love.

Don't know how to love.

They will only love
when their peers love.

Some people don't know
what to hate on.

How to hate on.

They will only hate
when their peers hate on something.

They preach goodness.
They preach holiness.

They preach to the people
in need

but only if you agree with them.

Only if you have
the same views.

Some people,
I swear,

they don't know

what to believe in

and they don't know
how to be themselves.

They just follow
because it is the only thing

they were taught
to do.

PEACE WITH MYSELF

I'm at peace
when you leave

because I know my heart.

I know who I am
and I don't let your chaos

get in the way.

THE RIGHT ONES

The right people
will always make you better.

They'll water your soul,
keep you grounded

and give you the kind of love
you need

and deserve.

IT IS OKAY

I'm realizing that
it's okay to take time

on myself.

That it's okay
to take things lightly

and not be in control
all the time.

That life
and love

always

start from giving.

And

letting go
and letting in

always

start from within.

PROTECT YOUR MAGIC

Sometimes
you have to move on

from the people you think
you love

and sometimes
you have to put

your well-being first…
no matter how bad it hurts.

So please,
don't be afraid to walk away

and don't be afraid
of starting over.

You must protect your heart
and your energy.

Always
and at all costs.

FLOWERS DIE TOO FAST

Flowers never pick themselves.

They pick us
and sadly,

we clip them off their stems
and kill them

to place them in our homes
for a week or two.

And it's the same way
with people.

We're never truly aware
of who we choose to love.

They just fall into our lives...
to change our lives

and from that moment on
we're never meant to be

the same.

Like the flower,
we're left to wilt

until our doom

over

our broken hearts.

Over

the broken possibility

and over

a love
that could have possibly

lasted forever
but instead,

lasted just enough
to urge us

to keep searching
for more.

OLD FEELINGS

And sometimes

old feelings will resurface
but you must understand

how moving on
is a process.

That sometimes
after so much progress

you're going to find yourself
back where you started.

No one ever said
healing was going to be easy.

Sometimes
you have to breakdown
to breakthrough.

Sometimes
you have to drown a little
before you find the courage

to swim toward the surface
again... to breathe again.

And sometimes
you're going to want to give in.

But I will tell you
to keep going.

To keep fighting.

To forgive
but not forget.

I know I've said this
countless times.

But you must move forward.

You must learn
how to progress.

Anything else
should be forgiven

or forgotten.

Anything else
was meant for you

to let go.

Nothing is forever.

And whatever is,

wasn't meant
for you to hold.

BLOOM

The right people

will make
loving yourself easy.

Even when it rains
they'll bring out the sun

and watch you
bloom.

THE BEST KIND

The best kind
of humans

are the ones
who fill the void

with laughter.

The ones
who make you feel

something familiar

and the ones
who always leave your heart

reaching
for a little more.

UNTAMED

The heart is stubborn.

Untameable.

It'll sometimes want
who's not for it

and leave
who'll keep it

alive.

YEARS AND YEARS

And it might take years
but the best thing

about patience is,

you always get
what you need.

You always get
what you ask for

and in the end,

you always get
what you deserve.

OUT OF MARGIN

There are some things
you just don't do

to the person you love.

Some things
you can't take back.

So be a little more careful
next time.

Treat them a little kinder
and hold on to their hearts

a little softer.

They deserve
the best version of you.

No games.
No lies.

No secrets
and no surprises.

Just be real with them,
know your place

and never get
out of line.

NO HURT HERE

You don't hurt someone
you want to keep.

You do them right
and let fate decide

who leaves
and who stays.

THE ANSWERS

The answers don't
reveal themselves overnight.

They take time
and they take as long

as they wish to manifest.

So stop overthinking.

Stop putting yourself
in that position of stress

and desperation.

One day it will all make sense.

One day
everything will connect for you

and you will realize
how everything that hurt

had to happen

to make you
the person

you currently are.

I promise.

NOT JUST

It's not just the women
who get hurt.

Who get cheated on.

Who feel like dying
when they feel most alone.

Sometimes
the men feel this way, too

and sadly,
some of them go unheard.

Some of them
hold the pain in

because they don't want
to seem vulnerable.

They don't want
to seem weak.

Like women,
men also need someone

who understands.

Someone to hold them—
to care for them.

And someone
who could make sense

of the way they feel

without the use

of words.

HANG IN THERE

Hang in there.

Everything you're going through
will pass.

Everything is preparing you
for what you need

and not
what you want.

Know the difference.

The people who've done you wrong
are making way

for the people
who'll do you right.

Be patient.

Love is real
and know...

how everything will work
itself out

in the end.

It always has
and always will.

Just hang in there

everything soon
will make sense.

HOW FAR YOU HAVE COME

Remind yourself
of how far you've come.

Look at your past.
Look at your pain.

Look at everytime you thought
it was the end.

It wasn't, right?

And you didn't die...
you overcame what hurts.

And yes,
you've lost a few people

but look at you now,
you're stronger,

healthier
and trying to make sense
of it all.

You're a goddamn miracle
and every chance you get

you're making wine

out of water.

I salute you
for your courage,

it inspires me...

and I hope
the love you harbor within

doesn't change for no one...
not even for the things
you love.

Keep soaring
and keep doing

what you do.

STILL CARE

Sometimes

you have to tell people
when you miss them.

You have to let them know
how you feel

and let them know
how much

you still care.

STRONGER THAN BEFORE

You're strong
because you left someone

who did you wrong
and it was someone

you never thought
you'd leave.

That's a brave thing
to do.

To look beyond
what you want

and chase
what you need.

Follow your heart.

POETRY

Poetry can sometimes heal
some of the deepest wounds.

Poetry can sometimes save you
and hold you

when you need it most.

PEACE TO LET GO

It is bringing me peace
to let go

of the people
I thought I once needed.

It is bringing me growth
and experience.

Because I have come
to the conclusion

that I do not need
a thousand friends.

I just need a few
and if we are still friends

after all this time...

then that obviously means
something.

It means
I need you more

than I think I do
and I am grateful

we have made it
this long.

WAY YOU FEEL

It hurts when you feel empty
and can't explain why.

That's the worse kind
of sadness.

You feel it deeply
all over your soul

and you can never
understand

why you feel
the way you feel.

THE SCIENCE BEHIND HEALING

You're still trying to heal
from all the things

you can't explain
and that's what makes you

so goddamn beautiful.

You take the stars
and create universes

without fully understanding

the science
behind how they work.

THEY JUST DO NOT KNOW

You have to keep doing
what you're doing

and ignore
the people who keep judging you...

because most of them
don't know how to live.

Most of them
only judge others

to justify
what they don't know

about themselves.

IT IS SAD

It is sad
when you have to pretend

you don't care.

You hold the door for them
as they pass through

without having the courage

to say

what it is
you feel.

ONE OF THE...

One of the worst things
you can ever do...

is

feel like you've wasted
your time,

your love,
your energy
and your soul

on someone
who didn't deserve it

from the start.

THE CAR RIDE

A long car ride home
with someone you love,

can sometimes heal you
in ways

you can't *imagine.*

WAITING FOR

You ask me
what I am waiting for?

I'm waiting for someone
who keeps it real.

For someone
who doesn't make a fool

out of me
and plays with my heart—

for someone grown.

I don't have time for people
who don't fuel my soul.

For people who don't bring the light.

I'm sorry, I'm just waiting for someone
who'll treat me

like a fucking human being
and not take

what I have to offer for granted.

That's all.

TAKE YOUR TIME

Take your time
if you want it to last.

Don't rush into it.

A garden doesn't grow overnight.

You patiently plant
each flower at a time

and feed it love
and water

until it grows.

And it's the same with people
and relationships.

You give them a chance.
You give them respect.

You give them understanding
and loyalty and love...

and soon enough
it blooms into something beautiful.

Into something

you need

and something
you know

you'll never have the

heart

to let go.

ONLY IF THEY LOVE YOU

If they love you
they won't give up on you.

They will forgive you
and fight for you.

No matter how tragic
the relationship gets.

PART OF YOUR LIFE

If they want to be
a part of your life

they will put the effort in.

They won't miss your call.
They won't go back on their word.

They won't ignore you
for someone else.

And they definitely won't
disappoint you or break your trust.

If someone wants you,
they'll do whatever it takes

to make things work
for the best

and they'll do so...
carefully.

They'll give you wings
if you're afraid to fall

and they'll drink the ocean
if you're afraid to swim.

They'll put the effort in
and do whatever it takes...

to make you feel
at home.

WE MUST

And we don't
ever really know

if we have enough
within us

to move on

but we *do*
because we *can*

because we *must*.

THE PROBLEM

That's the problem.

Some people
tend to care

when they can no longer
do anything about it.

When you've already moved on
and when you've already

learned

how to be
on your own.

DO NOT PRETEND

You don't have to pretend
to be busy because you're hurt.

You don't have to pretend
you don't care.

It's okay to be vulnerable sometimes.

It's okay to show
what's in your heart.

Some of the strongest people
I know express themselves

with no fear.

It's okay to cry—
to let it all out.

The rain cleanses.
The storm floods.

And in the end,
you're reborn into a different kind

of human
with a different kind

of energy,

and a different kind
of love.

GETS REAL

You'll know who to keep
when shit gets real.

So stay away
from fake love,

keep your eyes open
and don't break your own heart

chasing everything
you hear.